D1280082

BASKETBALL
TRIVIA

By Phil Ervin

GOLDEN STATE
30
WAR ORS

SportsZone

An Imprint of Abdo Publishing
abdopublishing.com

abdopublishing.com

Published by Abdo Publishing, a division of ABDO, PO Box 398166, Minneapolis, Minnesota 55439. Copyright © 2016 by Abdo Consulting Group, Inc. International copyrights reserved in all countries. No part of this book may be reproduced in any form without written permission from the publisher. SportsZone™ is a trademark and logo of Abdo Publishing.

Printed in the United States of America, North Mankato, Minnesota
082015
012016

Cover Photo: Rick Scuteri/AP Images
Interior Photos: Rick Scuteri/AP Images, 1, 4; Reed Saxon/AP Images, 7; AP Images, 9, 19 (right), 31, 40; John Gaps/AP Images, 11; Michael Perez/AP Images, 13; Mark J. Terrill/AP Images, 14, 29; Charles Krupa/AP Images, 17; Dean Bertoncelj/Shutterstock Images, 19 (left); Clifford Ginsburg/Bettmann/Corbis, 21; Paul Sancya/AP Images, 22; Tony Avelar/AP Images, 25; Bob Child/AP Images, 27; HF/AP Images, 32; Tim Johnson/AP Images, 35; Bob Galbraith/AP Images, 37; Tom Pidgeon/AP Images, 39; Charles Knoblock/AP Images, 42

Editor: Patrick Donnelly
Series Designer: Jake Nordby

Library of Congress Control Number: 2015945763

Cataloging-in-Publication Data
Ervin, Phil.
 Basketball trivia / Phil Ervin.
   p. cm. -- (Sports trivia)
 ISBN 978-1-68078-002-4 (lib. bdg.)
 Includes bibliographical references and index.
 1. Basketball--Miscellanea--Juvenile literature.   2. Sports--Miscellanea--Juvenile literature.   I. Title.
 796.323--dc23

2015945763

CONTENTS

Basketball was invented in the late 1800s. Since then it has gained popularity throughout the world. The National Basketball Association (NBA) is one of the world's most-watched professional sports leagues. Millions of fans also watch the National Collegiate Athletic Association (NCAA) tournaments. And basketball is a popular part of the Summer Olympics.

This book does not contain all there is to know about basketball. But it does feature some of the sport's most interesting facts, figures, and stories. Read on to find out more about them.

*All statistics and answers current through the 2014–15 NBA and NCAA basketball seasons.

CHAPTER 1

ROOKIE

Q **Which NBA player has won the most Most Valuable Player (MVP) Awards?**

A Kareem Abdul-Jabbar was named the NBA's MVP a record six times. Abdul-Jabbar was a star center for the Milwaukee Bucks and Los Angeles Lakers. In his 20-year career, he won six NBA championships. He also was twice named the NBA Finals MVP.

Q **Who invented basketball?**

A A schoolteacher named Dr. James Naismith is the father of the sport. Naismith invented a game called "Basket Ball" in Springfield, Massachusetts, in 1891. In the first

Kareem Abdul-Jabbar, *left*, launches a hook shot over Seattle's Xavier McDaniel in 1989.

games, peach baskets were hung at opposite ends of the gymnasium. Players threw soccer balls into them. Naismith wrote 13 rules for the game. It evolved into modern-day basketball.

Q Who is the NBA's all-time leading three-point shooter?

A Ray Allen made 2,973 three-pointers in 18 NBA seasons. Allen also is the NBA's all-time leader in three-point attempts. He made 40 percent of his shots from beyond the arc.

Q Who is men's college basketball's all-time leading scorer?

A Pete Maravich holds that record. His nickname was "Pistol Pete" because he liked to shoot. He scored a total of 3,667 points in 83 college games. That is an average of 44.2 points per game. Maravich played only three years of college basketball at Louisiana State University (LSU). And he played before the three-point line was used. But his NCAA record still stands.

A The Boston Celtics lead all teams with 17 league titles. Their history includes eight consecutive championships from 1959 to 1966. The Lakers rank second with 16 titles. They won 11 after moving to Los Angeles in 1959. The team won its first five when it played in Minneapolis. The Chicago Bulls are third with six championships.

Q Which country has won the most Olympic gold medals in basketball?

A The United States has dominated Olympic basketball competition. The US men have won 14 gold medals. Their first came in 1936. That was the first year basketball was played in the Olympics. Women's basketball was introduced in 1976. Team USA has won seven of the ten gold medals through 2012. The only other country that has won more than one gold medal in either men's or women's hoops is the Soviet Union.

Michael Jordan, *left*, Patrick Ewing, *center*, and Scottie Pippen helped Team USA win another gold medal in 1992.

Q **Which college has won the most men's NCAA championships?**

A The University of California, Los Angeles (UCLA), has won 11 national titles. All but one of them came in a 12-season stretch from 1964–75. Basketball Hall of Famer John Wooden was the Bruins' coach during that era. They added their twelfth title in 1995.

Q Who is the NBA's all-time leading scorer?

A Kareem Abdul-Jabbar scored 38,387 points during his 20 NBA seasons. Karl Malone, Kobe Bryant, and Michael Jordan are next on the all-time scoring list. When he retired in 1989, Abdul-Jabbar also led the league in blocked shots and seasons played.

Q How many times has a Number 16 seed upset a Number 1 seed in the NCAA men's basketball tournament?

A Zero. The tournament expanded to 64 teams in 1985. Since then, Number 16 seeds are 0-124 against Number 1 seeds. However, seven Number 15 seeds have upset Number 2 seeds in the first round. It happened twice in 2012. That year Norfolk State beat Missouri, and Lehigh defeated Duke. In 2013 Florida Gulf Coast upset Georgetown.

Q Which coach has won the most NBA championships?

A Phil Jackson won 11 championships as a coach. His Chicago Bulls won six titles in the 1990s. Jackson then moved to Los Angeles and won five more with the Lakers. He was inducted into the Basketball Hall of Fame in 2007.

Q In 2012, six of the 12 players on the US Women's Olympic basketball team came from the same college. Can you name it?

A Connecticut players made up half of the US roster that year. It should not be a surprise. The Huskies have dominated women's college basketball. They have won 10 national titles, nine of them since 2000. And the US team was coached by Geno Auriemma, who also coaches at Connecticut.

WHICH PLAYER WAS SELECTED TO THE ALL-NBA FIRST TEAM THE MOST?

You might think it was Michael Jordan. But it was not. Longtime Utah Jazz forward Karl Malone did it 11 times. So did Lakers guard Kobe Bryant. Malone retired in 2004 after playing with Bryant for one season in Los Angeles. Jordan was named to the All-NBA first team 10 times.

CHAPTER 2

VETERAN

Q Who is the only person to have been honored as the NBA's top player, coach, and executive?

A Larry Bird left his mark on professional basketball like few others. Bird was named the NBA's MVP three seasons in a row in the mid-1980s as a member of the Boston Celtics. As coach of the Indiana Pacers he earned Coach of the Year honors in 1997–98. And as the Pacers' team president, Bird was named the NBA's Executive of the Year in 2011–12.

Q Which NCAA men's champion was the first to feature an all-black starting lineup?

Larry Bird lived up to his nickname—
Legend—in many ways.

A Texas Western coach Don Haskins made history in 1966. In a time when some colleges still did not recruit black athletes, Haskins started five black players in the national championship game. Texas Western beat top-ranked (and all-white) Kentucky 72–65. Three years later, Kentucky became one of the last major college teams to begin recruiting black players.

Q Which former player's outline can be seen in the NBA's logo?

A Los Angeles Lakers guard Jerry West is the man in the iconic image. Designer Alan Siegel found a picture of West and turned it into the official NBA logo in 1969. West played for Los Angeles from 1960–74. He was an All-Star in each of those seasons. He also won the NBA Finals MVP Award in 1969.

Q How many varsity games did Michael Jordan play as a sophomore in high school?

A He did not play at all for the varsity team. But he did play for the junior varsity team that year. According to

a popular myth, Jordan was cut from the Laney High School team his sophomore year. In reality Jordan was just like a lot of other high school players. He had to work hard and wait his turn. He made varsity as a junior.

Q Who is the NBA's all-time leader in triple-doubles?

A Former star point guard Jason Kidd holds the record with 107. A triple-double involves a player recording double-digit totals in three key statistical categories in a game. Usually it covers points, rebounds, and assists. But a player also could have 10 or more steals or blocked shots in a game.

Q Which US basketball players have won the most Olympic gold medals?

A US women's team members Teresa Edwards and Lisa Leslie are tied with four each. No male basketball player has won more than two gold medals.

Q Who are the shortest and tallest players to play in an NBA game?

A At 5 feet 3 inches, guard Tyrone "Muggsy" Bogues is the shortest. On the other end, center Manute Bol was 7 feet 7 inches tall. The two were teammates on the 1987–88 Washington Bullets. Former NBA center Gheorghe Muresan also was 7 feet 7 inches tall. He played for Washington and the New Jersey Nets from 1993–2000.

Q How long was the longest winning streak in NBA history?

A The 1971–72 Los Angeles Lakers won 33 games in a row. Then they won the 1972 NBA title. That team also had a 69–13 regular-season record.

The Washington Bullets had both extremes represented with Manute Bol, *left*, and Tyrone Bogues in the lineup.

Only one team has ever won more games in a season. Eight NBA teams have won at least 19 games in a row in one season. The Atlanta Hawks did it in 2014–15.

Q How long was the longest losing streak in NBA history?

A In 2010–11 the Cleveland Cavaliers lost 26 games in a row. The Philadelphia 76ers matched the Cavs with 26 straight defeats in 2013–14.

Q Which college won the Division I men's and women's national championships in the same year?

WHICH NBA PLAYER HAS WON THE MOST DEFENSIVE PLAYER OF THE YEAR AWARDS?

Two players are tied for this honor. Detroit Pistons big man Ben Wallace won his fourth Defensive Player of the Year Award in 2005–06. That tied him with Dikembe Mutombo. The shot-blocking center won it four times with three different teams in the late 1990s and early 2000s.

A Connecticut has actually done it twice. The Huskies men and women won it all in 2004. Then they did it again in 2014.

Q Which player has won the most NBA championships?

A Former Boston Celtics great Bill Russell has more championship rings than fingers. The center played on 11 NBA Finals-winning teams during his 13-year career from 1956–69. Russell earned MVP honors in five of those seasons. He is also the league's second-leading rebounder of all time.

Q Which NBA player holds the record for three-pointers made in a season?

A Golden State gunner Stephen Curry set that record during the 2014–15 season. Curry made 286 three-pointers, breaking his own NBA record of 272 set in 2012–13. Curry has three of the top five three-point shooting seasons in league history.

CHAPTER 3

CHAMPION

Q Who are the only women's college basketball players to be named first-team All-Americans four years in a row?

A Courtney Paris of Oklahoma was the first to do it. She played for the Sooners from 2005–09. Connecticut star Maya Moore matched Paris two years later.

Q When was the three-point line invented?

A The American Basketball League introduced the three-point line 1961. That league folded after just 1 1/2 seasons. The American Basketball Association (ABA) adopted the three-point arc in 1967. The ABA folded in

Maya Moore of UConn is one of the most decorated college basketball players ever.

1976. Four of its teams joined the NBA. But the NBA did not add a three-point line until 1979.

A On March 2, 1962, Philadelphia Warriors center Wilt Chamberlain scored 100 points. The Warriors beat the New York Knicks 169–147. The team mark for points in a game came much later. On December 13, 1983, the Detroit Pistons beat the Denver Nuggets 186–184 in triple overtime. Those are the two highest single-team scores in NBA history.

A Nate Robinson is the only player to have won three dunk crowns. At 5 feet 9 inches, Robinson also is one of the shortest players ever to have participated. Yet he topped the field in 2006, 2009, and 2010 as a member of the New York Knicks. Spud Webb is the only shorter player

to have won the dunk contest. The 5-foot-6 guard for the Atlanta Hawks did it in 1986.

Q Which player averaged a triple-double for a season?

A Oscar Robertson of the Cincinnati Royals did it in 1961–62. "The Big O" averaged 30.8 points, 12.5 rebounds, and 11.4 assists per game that season.

A Three Number 11 seeds have accomplished the feat. LSU did it in 1986. Twenty years later, George Mason made it. And in 2011 Virginia Commonwealth joined the group. None of them reached the national championship game. In 1985 Villanova became the lowest seed to ever win a national title—the Wildcats were seeded eighth.

A Four teams have honored Wilt the Stilt. He played for three different NBA teams. Each one retired his No. 13 jersey. Chamberlain started with the Philadelphia Warriors. He stayed with them when the team moved to San Francisco. He then won NBA titles with the Philadelphia 76ers and Los Angeles Lakers. But before that, he played for a traveling team called the Harlem Globetrotters. They retired his No. 13 in 2000.

Q How many Number 1 overall draft picks have gone on to win the NBA MVP Award?

A Only 10 players who were drafted first overall have gone on to win NBA MVP honors. Eight of them did so after the NBA Draft Lottery was implemented in 1985.

Q How many NBA players have won Rookie of the Year and MVP honors in the same season?

A It has happened twice. Wilt Chamberlain earned Rookie
of the Year and MVP honors in 1959–60 during his first
season with the Philadelphia Warriors. Wes Unseld
did the same in 1968–69 as a center for the Baltimore
Bullets.

Q **Which NBA team had the most wins in a season?**

A The 1995–96 Bulls finished the regular season 72–10. That gave them the most wins in an NBA season. It also remains the highest regular-season winning percentage (.878) ever achieved. Led by Michael Jordan, that team went on to win the first of three straight NBA Finals.

HOW MANY NBA PLAYERS HAVE BEEN NAMED MVP, ALL-STAR GAME MVP, AND FINALS MVP IN THE SAME YEAR?

Michael Jordan, Shaquille O'Neal, and Willis Reed are the only three players to have accomplished this feat. Jordan did it twice—in 1996 and 1998—with the Bulls. O'Neal turned the trick in 2000 with the Los Angeles Lakers. But Reed was the first, winning all three awards with the New York Knicks in 1970.

CHAPTER 4

HALL OF FAMER

Q How many NBA players have produced a quadruple-double?

A It has only happened five times. Nate Thurmond of the Chicago Bulls had the first in 1974. Hakeem Olajuwon of the Houston Rockets did it twice in March 1990. And San Antonio's David Robinson pulled it off four years later. Those feats all included double figures in points, rebounds, assists, and blocked shots. Alvin Robertson of the Spurs took a different route in a 1986 game. Instead of blocked shots, he had 10 steals.

Q When did the first women's professional basketball league begin play?

Hakeem Olajuwon, *left*, was a shot-blocking force for the Houston Rockets.

A The Women's Professional Basketball League started in 1978. Its first game took place on December 9, 1978. The Chicago Hustle played against the Milwaukee Does. That league lasted three seasons. The Women's National Basketball Association (WNBA) began play in 1997.

Q Which NBA coach has the most wins without an NBA championship?

A Jerry Sloan ranks third on the NBA's all-time wins list with 1,221. However, none of those victories earned any of his teams a title. Sloan's Utah Jazz teams reached the NBA Finals in 1997 and 1998. But both years they lost to Michael Jordan and the Bulls. Sloan coached the Bulls from 1979–82 and the Jazz from 1988–2011.

Q Which two leagues merged to form the NBA?

A The Basketball Association of America (BAA) began play in 1946. It was a rival to the National Basketball League (NBL). The BAA had teams in big cities. The NBL had most of the best players. The two merged in time for the 1949–50 season. The Minneapolis Lakers won the first NBA title that season.

Jerry Sloan was a Hall of Fame coach who never won an NBA championship.

Q How many players have won an Olympic gold medal, an NCAA championship, and an NBA title?

A Seven players belong to this exclusive group. Some names are immediately recognizable: Michael Jordan, Magic Johnson, and Bill Russell. Others might be less familiar to younger fans. But Clyde Lovellette, K. C. Jones, Quinn Buckner, and Jerry Lucas all were stars in their day.

Q Which NBA player has played for the most teams?

A Four have played for 12 teams. Forward Chucky Brown became the first when he signed with the Sacramento Kings in 2002. Guard Jim Jackson, forward Tony Massenburg, and forward Joe Smith also played for 12 different teams.

Q In what other sport did Spurs big man Tim Duncan excel as a child?

A Duncan has won five NBA championships and two NBA MVP Awards. Before that he was on track to become an Olympic swimmer. However, Hurricane Hugo hit the US Virgin Islands in 1989. The storm destroyed the pool where Duncan swam. His only alternative was to swim in the ocean. But he was afraid of sharks. So Duncan focused on basketball and became a star.

Q Who is the oldest player to have played in an NBA or BAA game?

A Nat Hickey coached the BAA's Providence Steamrollers in 1947–48. Late in the season, Hickey inserted himself as a player. He was 45. It did not go very well. Hickey missed all six shots he took and committed five fouls.

Q Which sports did Patrick Ewing play before basketball?

A Growing up in Kingston, Jamaica, the former New York Knicks center preferred cricket and soccer. Basketball is not as popular as other sports there. But when Ewing

WHO IS THE ONLY PLAYER TO HAVE WON MVP HONORS IN BOTH THE NBA AND ABA?

Julius "Dr. J" Erving was one of the ABA's most popular players. Then he became one of the NBA's most popular players. He was named the ABA MVP three times and the NBA MVP once.

discovered hoops, he quickly fell in love with the game. In college Ewing was a three-time All-American and led Georgetown to the 1984 NCAA championship. He then went on to play 17 years in the NBA, 15 of them with the New York Knicks. Ewing was an 11-time All-Star and a member of the 1992 US Olympic "Dream Team" that won the gold medal in Barcelona, Spain.

A When George Mikan started playing for the Minneapolis Lakers, he changed the game. Basketball was originally considered a sport for shorter people. To prevent the 6-foot-10 Mikan from completely overrunning the league, the NBA changed some of its rules. The most notable change was goaltending. This bars a player from blocking a shot while the ball is above the rim.

Q How many NBA players are in the "50–40–90" club?

A Ten players have achieved this feat. A "50–40–90" season means a player had an incredible year shooting the ball. The numbers refer to shooting at least 50 percent from the field, 40 percent on three-pointers, and 90 percent from the free throw line. Former star point guard Steve Nash did it an NBA-record four times with the Phoenix Suns.

TRIVIA QUIZ

1 LeBron James was a high school star in basketball and which other sport?

a. football

b. basketball

c. baseball

d. tennis

2 Who is the all-time leading scorer in NBA playoff history?

a. Kareem Abdul-Jabbar

b. Larry Bird

c. Magic Johnson

d. Michael Jordan

3 For which of the following teams has Kevin Garnett not played?

a. Minnesota Timberwolves

b. Boston Celtics

c. Brooklyn Nets

d. Milwaukee Bucks

4 Which NBA team allowed the fewest points per game in a season?

a. 1998–99 Atlanta Hawks

b. 1998–99 Miami Heat

c. 1994–95 Atlanta Hawks

d. 2003–04 San Antonio Spurs

5 Which WNBA team has won the most championships?

a. Minnesota Lynx

c. Houston Comets

b. Los Angeles Sparks

d. Phoenix Mercury

6 Which NBA point guard's nickname was The Houdini of the Hardwood?

a. John Stockton

c. Gary Payton

b. Bob Cousy

d. Oscar Robertson

7 Who is the leading scorer in ABA history?

a. Julius Erving

c. Ron Boone

b. Louie Dampier

d. Mack Calvin

8 In which year did men's basketball become an official Olympic event?

a. 1948

c. 1936

b. 1976

d. 1928

9 Which of these four teams was not an original member of the NBA?

a. Anderson Packers

c. Seattle SuperSonics

b. Waterloo Hawks

d. Washington Capitols

*Answers on page 47

GLOSSARY

accolade
An award, honor, or praise.

distinction
A trait or characteristic that sets someone or something apart.

draft
The process by which leagues determine which teams will sign new players coming into the league.

full-court press
A defensive strategy in which defenders closely guard the player with the ball for the entire length of the court.

goaltending
Touching the ball when it is above the rim.

quadruple-double
A game in which a player has a double-digit total in four different categories (points, rebounds, assists, steals, or blocked shots).

recruit
Convince a high school player to attend a college, usually to play sports.

seed
The ranking of a team in a tournament.

FOR MORE INFORMATION

Books

Frisch, Nate. *The Story of the Golden State Warriors*.
Mankato, MN: Creative Education, 2015.

Norwich, Grace. *I Am LeBron James*. New York: Scholastic
Paperbacks, 2014.

Williams, Doug. *Great Moments in Olympic Basketball*.
Minneapolis, MN: Abdo Publishing, 2015.

Websites

To learn more about Sports Trivia, visit
booklinks.abdopublishing.com. These links are routinely
monitored and updated to provide the most current
information available.

Answers

1. a   6. b
2. d   7. b
3. d   8. c
4. a   9. c
5. c

INDEX

About the Author

Phil Ervin is a freelance sportswriter who lives in Minneapolis, Minnesota. He was born and raised in Omaha, Nebraska. In the past, he has written for Fox Sports North, the St. Joseph (Missouri) News-Press, and the Forsyth County (Georgia) News. Phil attended Benedictine College in Atchison, Kansas.